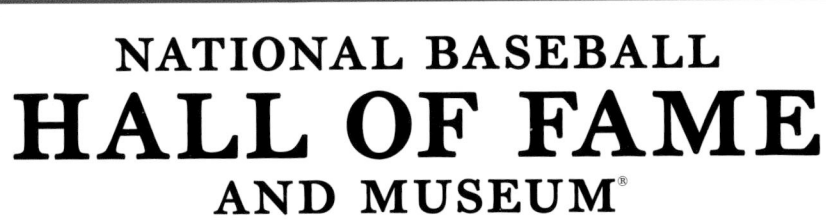

# NATIONAL BASEBALL
# HALL OF FAME
## AND MUSEUM®

=== MAP&GUIDE ===

D1215681

NATIONAL
★ ★ ★ ★ ★
BASEBALL
HALL OF FAME

This edition © 2014 Scala Arts Publishers, Inc.
Text © The National Baseball Hall of Fame and Museum
Pictures © The National Baseball Hall of Fame Library, Cooperstown, New York

Published by
Scala Arts Publishers, Inc.
141 Wooster Street, Suite 4D
New York, NY 10012
www.scalapublishers.com

ISBN-13: 978-1-85759-904-6
First published in 2006
Revised editions published in 2008 and 2014

Design and Project Management: Benjamin Shaykin
Copy Editor: Eleanor Hampton
Printed in China
10 9 8 7 6 5 4 3

Page 1: Opening day at the National Baseball Hall of Fame and Museum, June 12, 1939
This page: Uniform worn by Babe Ruth

# Contents

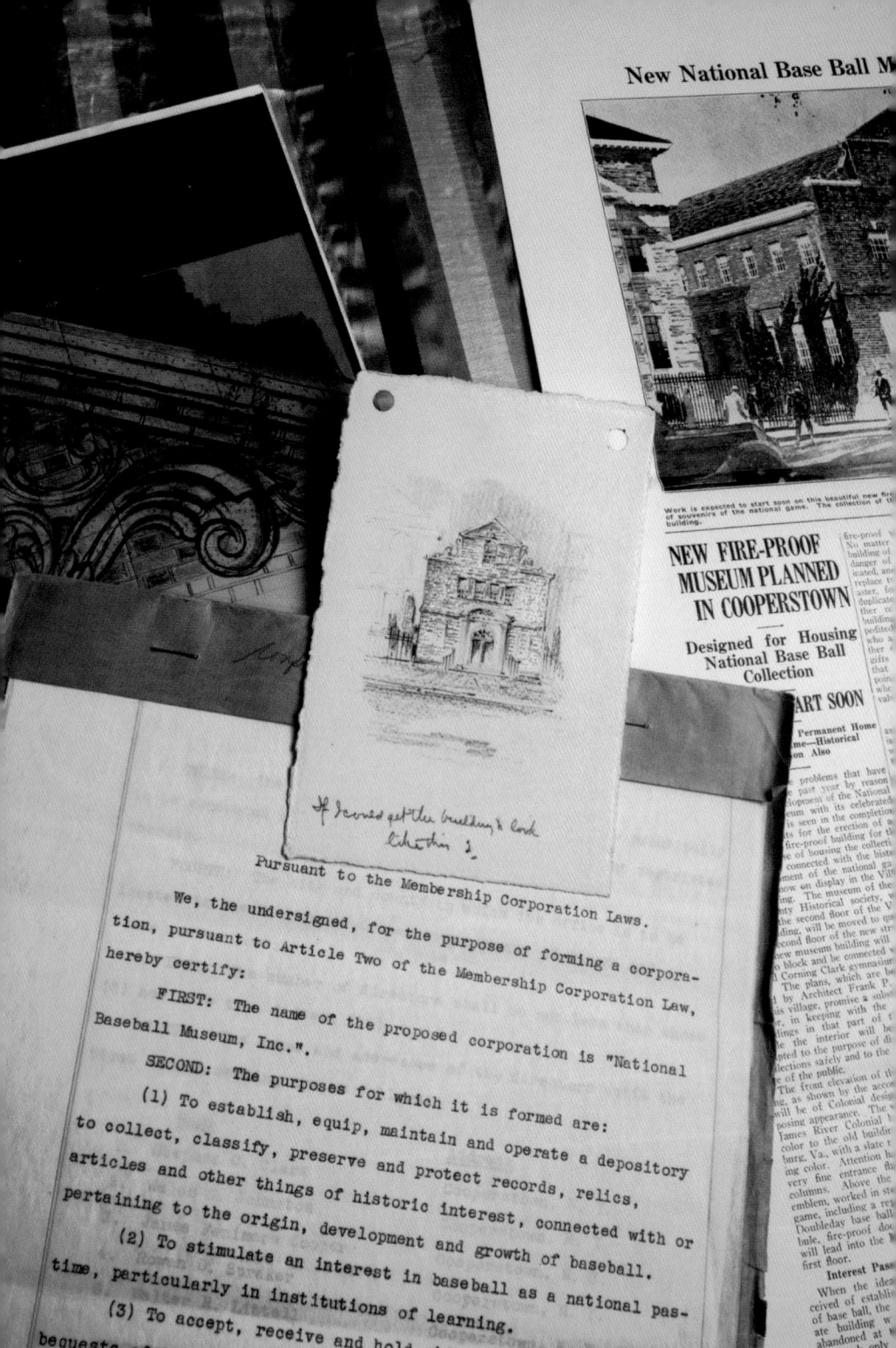

**NEW FIRE-PROOF MUSEUM PLANNED IN COOPERSTOWN**

Designed for Housing National Base Ball Collection

*If I succeed get the building to look like this ?*

Pursuant to the Membership Corporation Laws.

We, the undersigned, for the purpose of forming a corporation, pursuant to Article Two of the Membership Corporation Law, hereby certify:

FIRST: The name of the proposed corporation is "National Baseball Museum, Inc.".

SECOND: The purposes for which it is formed are:

(1) To establish, equip, maintain and operate a depository to collect, classify, preserve and protect records, relics, articles and other things of historic interest, connected with or pertaining to the origin, development and growth of baseball.

(2) To stimulate an interest in baseball as a national pastime, particularly in institutions of learning.

(3) To accept, receive and hold gifts, contributions and bequests of money, of personal property, and devises of real property, in connection therewith; to invest and reinvest the same or the proceeds thereof, in securities

# Foreword

Cooperstown was founded in 1786. A visit today still feels like a step back in time: a single stop light, an idyllic Main Street, mom-and-pop shops, and vibrant-colored geraniums hanging from antique-style light posts in a tranquil environment. It's almost as if you've stepped into a Norman Rockwell painting when you enter the village that was first made famous by author James Fenimore Cooper.

The Museum, which sits dignified, yet understated, on Main Street, opened its doors on June 12, 1939. It started as a one-room gallery, but after several renovations, including a complete redesign less than a decade ago, the National Baseball Hall of Fame and Museum is now a state-of-the art learning center and an important part of the landscape that helps define the culture of baseball.

Some 16 million visitors have made the pilgrimage and entered the three-story red brick building expecting to discover the past, but instead actively relive their own experiences and personal history. Through engaging exhibits featuring artifacts, photographs, and stories, visitors experience a trip back in time they can share with family and friends.

Three entities reside under one roof: a Hall of Fame, which honors the game's greatest players, managers, umpires and executives; an education center, where tens of thousands of school children, on site and through technology in their own classrooms, learn how baseball and America have grown up together; and a Museum and Library, which houses the greatest collection and archive in the history of sports.

The collections run deep, and grow everyday, as history unfolds. In Cooperstown, the history of our game is literally at your fingertips and ever-changing.

From exhibit galleries hosting topics ranging from baseball's glorious records, to the history of World Series memorable moments to the stars of today's game, to cultural explorations including the Latino and African-American influence, to women's leagues to baseball's leading role in the desegregation of America, Cooperstown has it all.

As you stroll through the Museum, you can't help but marvel at some of the game's most compelling stories and iconic moments. There's so much from your childhood, and then some. You'll find it all, at the National Baseball Hall of Fame and Museum. Only in Cooperstown.

With warm regards,

Jeff Idelson
President
National Baseball Hall
of Fame and Museum

# Why Cooperstown?

## The Origins of the National Baseball Hall of Fame and Museum

From humble beginnings, the National Baseball Hall of Fame and Museum has become one of the nation's most recognizable and popular educational institutions. The Museum is located in the pastoral village of Cooperstown in central New York State, nestled between the Catskill and Adirondack mountains, 70 miles west of Albany, the state capital.

The Baseball Hall of Fame officially opened its doors on June 12, 1939. Cooperstown represents a step back in time, with buildings dating to the early nineteenth century and street-front shops right out of the 1950s. Some 300,000 people travel to the village each year to pay tribute to our national pastime by visiting the Hall of Fame, an institution that honors excellence, preserves history, and connects generations.

The most popular question asked by baseball enthusiasts making their pilgrimage to the spiritual home of the game is, "Why Cooperstown?" The answer involves a commission, a tattered baseball, a philanthropist, and a centennial celebration.

## The Mills Commission

The Mills Commission was appointed in 1905 to determine the origin of baseball. Albert G. Spalding, one of the game's pioneers, urged the formation of the committee following an article by Henry Chadwick, a famous early baseball writer, who contended that the sport evolved from the English game of rounders.

Seven prominent men comprised the commission. They were Col. A. G. Mills of New York, who played baseball before and during the Civil War and was the fourth president of the National League (1882–1884); Morgan G. Bulkeley, former governor and then U.S. senator of Connecticut, who served as the National League's first president in 1876; Arthur P. Gorman, U.S. senator from Maryland, a former player and former president of the National Baseball Club of Washington; Nicholas E. Young of Washington, D.C., a longtime player who was the first secretary and later the fifth president of the National League (1884–1902); Alfred J. Reach of Philadelphia and George Wright of Boston, both well-known businessmen and two of the most famous players of their day; and the president of the Amateur Athletic Union, James E. Sullivan of New York.

During its three-year study, the committee was deluged with communications on the subject. In support of the claim that Abner Doubleday invented the game, the testimony of Abner Graves, a mining engineer from Denver, figured prominently in the committee's inquiry.

Graves considered Doubleday an American hero. Doubleday had been appointed to the U.S. Military Academy at West Point, graduating in 1842. Subsequently, he served in the U.S.-Mexican War and the Civil War. According to

OPPOSITE: Artifacts and images from the opening of the National Baseball Hall of Fame and Museum, June 12, 1939.

historical records, he fired the first shot for the Union at Fort Sumter, South Carolina.

In his testimony, Graves claimed to have been present when Doubleday made changes to a local version of "town ball." As Graves described the game, one player tossed the ball straight in the air, allowing another player to hit the ball with a 4-inch-wide flat bat. Some twenty to fifty players, scattered about the field, attempted to catch the ball before the batter could run to a goal 50 feet away. According to Graves, Doubleday used a stick to mark out a diamond-shaped field in the dirt. His other refinements to the rudimentary game included limiting the number of players and adding four bases (hence, the name *baseball*).

The committee's final report, on December 30, 1907, stated, in part, that "the first scheme for playing baseball, according to the best evidence obtainable to date, was devised by Abner Doubleday at Cooperstown, N.Y. in 1839."

### The Baseball

The discovery of an old baseball in a dust-covered attic trunk in 1934 supported the committee's findings. The ball was located in a farmhouse in Fly Creek, a village three miles from Cooperstown, where the baseball—undersized, misshapen, and obviously homemade—was discovered. The stitched cover had been torn open, revealing stuffing of cloth instead of wool and cotton yarns, which comprise the interior of the modern baseball. The ball soon became known as the Doubleday Baseball.

### The Philanthropist

Soon after its discovery, the baseball was purchased for $5 by Stephen C. Clark, a Cooperstown resident and philanthropist. Clark conceived the idea of displaying the ball, along with such other baseball objects as could be obtained, in a room in the Village Club, which now houses the Cooperstown village library. The small one-room exhibition attracted tremendous

ABOVE: The Doubleday Baseball, from the mythical first game in 1839, found in an attic near Cooperstown in 1934. OPPOSITE: Abner Graves' letters to the Mills Commission.

public interest. With the assistance of Alexander Cleland, who had been associated with Clark in other endeavors, support was sought for the establishment of a national baseball museum.

Ford C. Frick, then president of the National League, was especially enthusiastic. He obtained the backing of Judge Kenesaw Mountain Landis, baseball's first commissioner, and William Harridge, president of the American League. Contributions and historically significant baseball memorabilia soon poured in from all parts of the country as word spread.

## Baseball's Centennial Celebration

Coincidentally, in 1935, plans were also being formulated for an appropriate celebration in Cooperstown to mark baseball's upcoming 100th anniversary, which would take place in 1939. Frick proposed that a hall of fame be established as part of the shrine to honor the game's immortals.

Members of the Baseball Writers' Association of America (BBWAA) were enlisted to select the greats who were to be honored. The first election was conducted in January 1936, and five players were selected—Ty Cobb, Babe Ruth, Honus Wagner, Christy Mathewson, and Walter Johnson.

The National Baseball Hall of Fame and Museum was officially dedicated on June 12, 1939. The game's four ranking executives of the period—Landis, Frick, Harridge, and William G. Bramham, president of the National Association of Professional Baseball Leagues—participated in the ribbon cutting. Of the twenty-five men who had been elected to the Hall of Fame to that point, eleven were still living, and each journeyed to Cooperstown to attend the centennial celebration. As part of the festivities, a baseball postage stamp commemorating the occasion was placed on sale that day at the Cooperstown Post Office, with Postmaster General James A. Farley presiding.

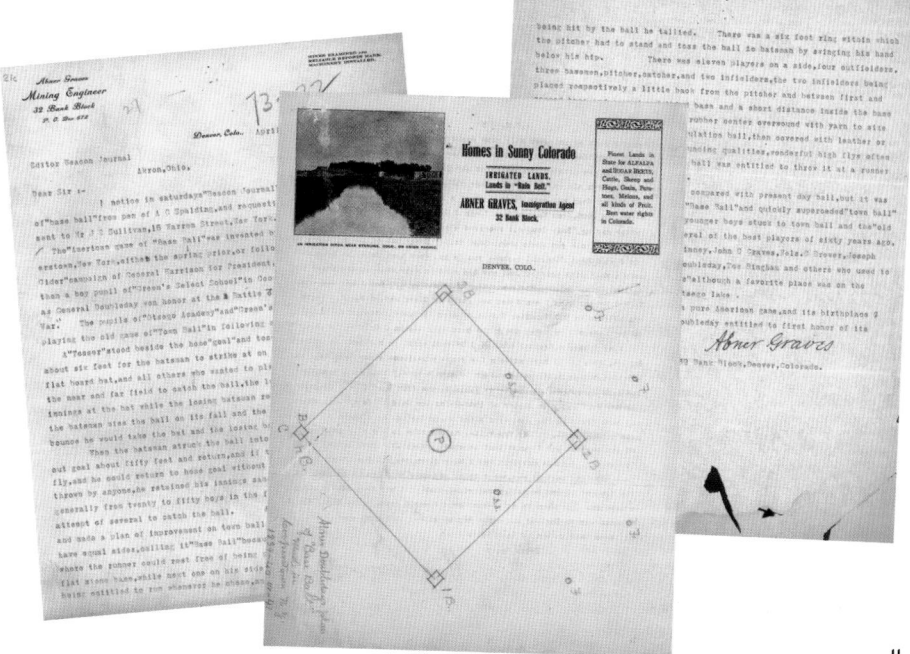

ABOVE: The first four classes of living inductees gathered for the opening of the Hall of Fame, June 12, 1939. Back row, left to right: Honus Wagner, Grover Cleveland Alexander, Tris Speaker, Nap Lajoie, George Sisler, and Walter Johnson. Front row, left to right: Eddie Collins, Babe Ruth, Connie Mack, and Cy Young. The eleventh living inductee, Ty Cobb, missed the photo due to travel delays. OPPOSITE: A pennant from the 1922 New York Yankees.

## New Research

After the commission reported its findings in 1908, many of the game's historians disputed Graves's account, noting that many of the innovations he attributed to Doubleday were already being practiced in the 1830s. The original Mills Commission papers, long thought to have been burned but finally discovered in 1999, support the view of many researchers that baseball developed from and along with other bat-and-ball games earlier in the eighteenth century. Cooperstown may not have been the point of origin for the game—that place likely does not exist—

but the game certainly evolved in pastoral settings like the idyllic Central New York village that now serves as home for baseball.

The Mills Commissions' contributions to our National Pastime is undeniable. By collecting the memories of many early fans and players while they were still living, the committee created a treasure trove of early baseball history that would otherwise have been lost. Moreover, by identifying Cooperstown as the site of the sport's origin, the Mills Commission initiated the process that ultimately established a home for the sport—the National Baseball Hall of Fame and Museum.

## Evolution of the
## Museum and Library

Since 1939, several significant enhancements have taken place at the Museum. Expansions in 1950 and 1980 added exhibit space, while the Hall of Fame Plaque Gallery was dedicated in 1958. In 1994, the original Library, which had opened in 1968, was renovated and connected to the Museum. In 2005, the Museum completed a three-year, $20 million renovation project to create a better experience for visitors, provide smoother traffic flow through the Museum's galleries, upgrade the environment for artifact preservation, and provide a greater presence of interactive technology for visitors.

Representing all aspects of baseball—both on the field and in our culture—the Museum collections total 40,000 three-dimensional artifacts (including bats, balls, gloves, caps, helmets, uniforms, shoes, trophies, and awards) and 135,000 baseball cards. All artifacts in the Museum's collections have been donated.

Founded in 1939 as part of the National Baseball Hall of Fame and Museum, the National Baseball Library is the largest repository of baseball information in the world. The Library is responsible for the acquisition, organization, preservation, and dissemination of all archival material related to the history of baseball and its impact on culture and society.

The National Baseball Library contains 2.6 million items that are housed in climate-controlled areas and maintained by a professional staff using state-of-the-art archival techniques. The photograph collection contains more than 250,000 historic images of players, teams, ballparks, and other baseball subjects. In addition, the Library's film, video, and recorded sound archives contain more than 14,000 hours of footage and audio recordings dating back to the late nineteenth century, including an extensive collection of Hollywood movies featuring baseball.

The Library is a public facility where numerous researchers and Museum visitors are served annually. While most patrons are independent baseball fans conducting research, others using the facilities have included such esteemed authors as George Plimpton, Roger Kahn, and George Will; officials from many major and minor league clubs; former big league players; writers from the *New York Times, USA Today,*

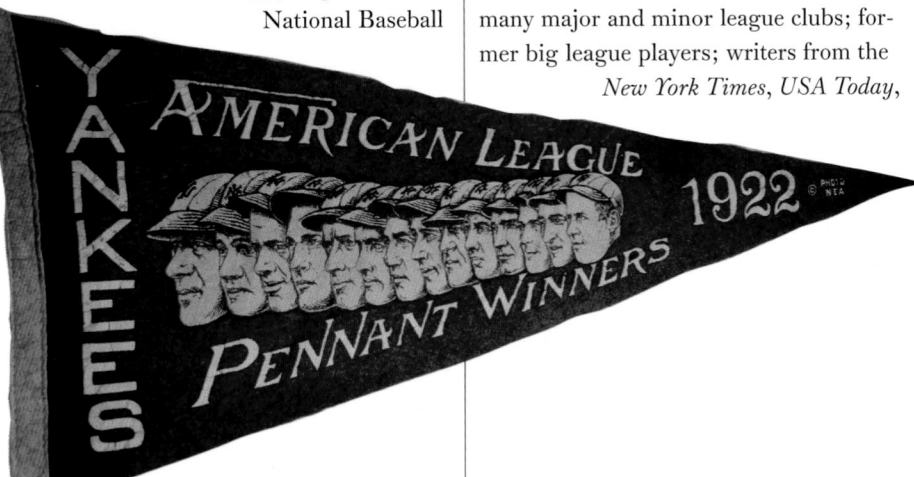

ABOVE: In 2002, twenty-four members of the Hall of Fame gathered at the American Museum of Natural History in New York City for the grand opening of Baseball As America. OPPOSITE TOP: Jane Forbes Clark, chairman, National Baseball Hall of Fame and Museum. OPPOSITE BELOW: Hall of Fame educators conduct a live videoconference from the Museum's second floor to students outside of Cooperstown.

and the *Wall Street Journal*; researchers from television shows such as *Jeopardy!*; and students of all ages. Whether it's simply answering a question or fielding a request from the White House for information for a presidential speech, the research department answers approximately 60,000 inquiries annually.

## The National Baseball Hall of Fame Today

In August 2000, the board of directors of the Museum elected the founder's granddaughter, Jane Forbes Clark, to be chairman. In 2008, Jeff Idelson became the Museum's sixth president. Under their leadership, the Museum has continued to broaden its educational outreach and has created an endowment to ensure its long-term financial security. In 2002, Baseball

As America, an exhibition of approximately 500 Museum artifacts, opened a six-year national tour to much acclaim at the American Museum of Natural History in New York City. The exhibit visited a total of fifteen world-class museums across the country during its run, which concluded in 2008. The national tour of *Baseball As America* was sponsored by Ernst & Young. Published by National Geographic, *Baseball As America: Seeing Ourselves Through Our National Game* is the official companion volume to the tour and is available for purchase at the Museum Bookstore.

The Hall of Fame's education programs extend the Museum's reach to children throughout the United States. The Museum's education team offers 17 thematic modules to students which explore subjects such as civil rights, mathematics and economics through the lens of baseball. In addition to on-site school visits, the Museum delivers interactive programs to classrooms outside Cooperstown via distance learning. The Museum's education outreach reaches tens of thousands of students through video-conferences each year.

As a part of its public programming for visitors of all ages, the Museum also offers an extensive year-round calendar of entertaining and informative events designed for families and baseball scholars alike. From roundtable discussions with Hall of Fame members to special event programs featuring staff and visiting experts highlighting baseball's rich history, to gallery talks, treasure hunts, concerts, movies, and plays, the Baseball Hall of Fame presents more than 1,000 educational events each year.

Additionally, Hall of Fame Weekend, featuring the annual Induction Ceremony and dozens of returning Hall of Fame members, highlights the year's schedule of events. Family entertainment, educational fundraisers, and unique baseball experiences take place year-round in Cooperstown. For those visitors unable to make frequent trips to Cooperstown, the Museum now offers exclusive content through baseballhall.org, ensuring many reasons to participate in baseball history all year long.

The Baseball Hall of Fame has become an international destination that chronicles the evolution of America's national pastime. From humble beginnings and a small collection of artifacts in the mid-1930s, the Hall of Fame has evolved into a cultural showcase, where people come to learn about the past and soon discover that baseball is the common thread of our national spirit.

Hall of Fame Plaque Gallery

TYRUS RAYMOND COBB
DETROIT-PHILADELPHIA, A.L.-1905-1928
LED AMERICAN LEAGUE IN BATTING
TWELVE TIMES AND CREATED OR
EQUALLED MORE MAJOR LEAGUE
RECORDS THAN ANY OTHER PLAYER.
RETIRED WITH 4191 MAJOR LEAGUE HITS.

WALTER PERRY JOHNS
WASHINGTON-1907-1927
CONCEDED TO BE FASTEST BALL
IN HISTORY OF GAME. WON 414
WITH LOSING TEAM BEHIND HIM MAN
HOLDER OF STRIKE OUT AND SHUT OUT

GEORGE HERMAN (BABE) RUTH
BOSTON-NEW YORK, A.L.; BOSTON, N.L.
1915-1935
GREATEST DRAWING CARD IN HISTORY OF
BASEBALL. HOLDER OF MANY HOME RUN
AND OTHER BATTING RECORDS. GATHERED
714 HOME RUNS IN ADDITION TO FIFTEEN
IN WORLD SERIES.

HONUS WAGNER
LOUISVILLE, N.L., 1897-1899.
PITTSBURGH, N.L., 1900-1917.
THE GREATEST SHORTSTOP IN BASEBALL
HISTORY. BORN CARNEGIE, PA., FEB. 24, 1874
KNOWN TO FAME AS "HONUS", "HANS" AND
"THE FLYING DUTCHMAN". RETIRED IN 1917,
HAVING SCORED MORE RUNS, MADE MORE
HITS AND STOLEN MORE BASES THAN
ANY OTHER PLAYER IN THE HISTORY
OF HIS LEAGUE

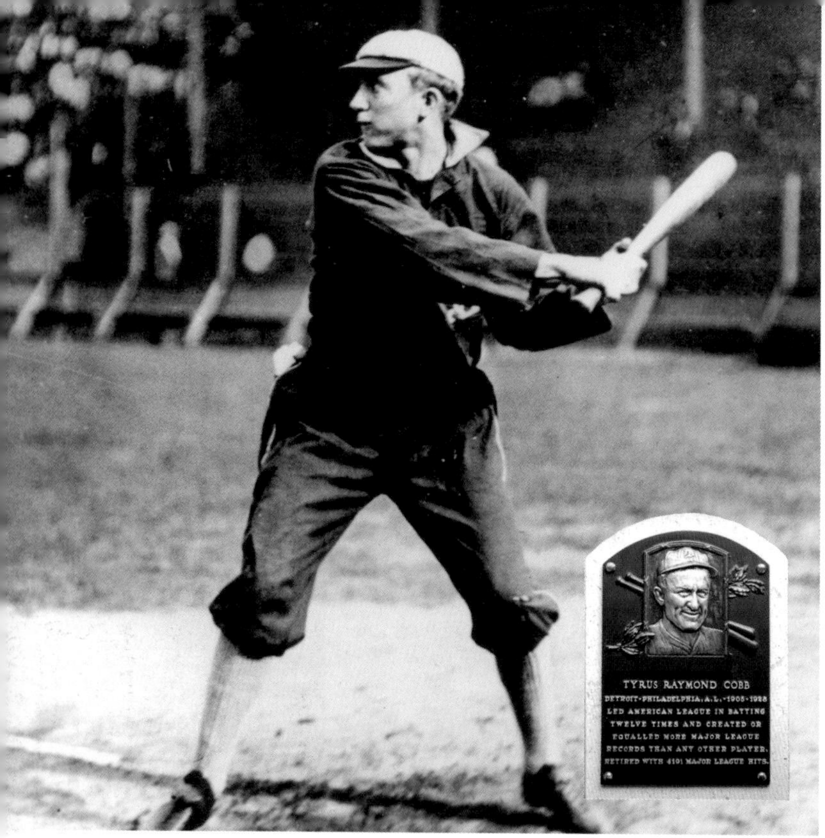

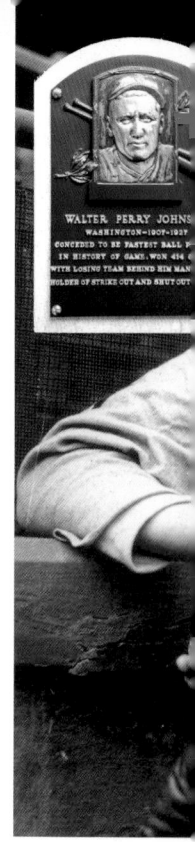

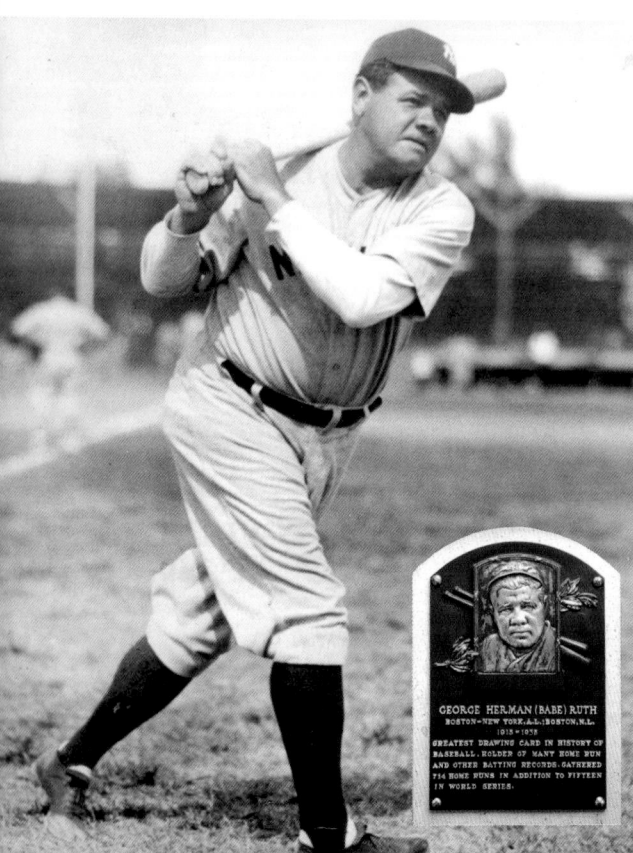

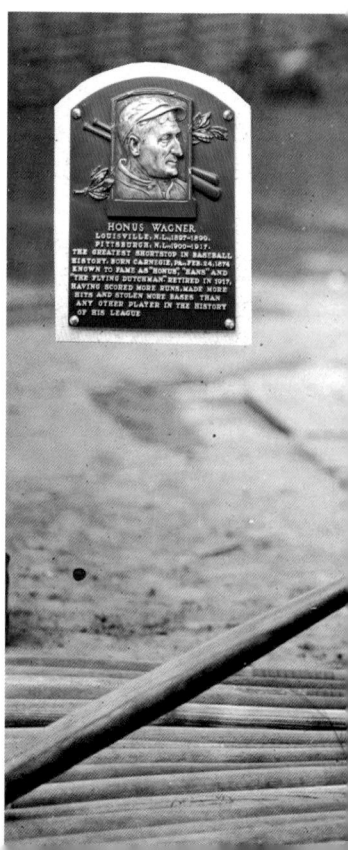

CHRISTY MATHEWSON
NEW YORK, N.L. 1900-1916.
CINCINNATI, N.L. 1916.
BORN FACTORYVILLE, PA., AUGUST 12, 1880
GREATEST OF ALL THE GREAT PITCHERS
IN THE 20TH CENTURY'S FIRST QUARTER
PITCHED 3 SHUTOUTS IN 1905 WORLD SERIES.
FIRST PITCHER OF THE CENTURY EVER TO
WIN 30 GAMES IN 3 SUCCESSIVE YEARS.
WON 37 GAMES IN 1908
"MATTY WAS MASTER OF THEM ALL"

# The First Five

Stroll through the Hall of Fame Plaque Gallery and stand among the game's greatest contributors. Each bronze plaque honors players, umpires, executives, and managers for their contributions to the game, from the first five electees in 1936—Babe Ruth, Walter Johnson, Christy Mathewson, Ty Cobb, and Honus Wagner—to the current class of inductees.

The Hall of Fame Plaque Gallery symbolizes the monumental odds of earning a place in Cooperstown. Just one player in every 100 talented enough to play in the major leagues earns a spot in the Hall of Fame.

The first class of plaques is displayed in the rotunda of the Gallery, with others placed by year of induction beginning on the right side.

Lockers feature artifacts from recent achievements for every major league team in *Today's Game*.

# Second Floor

# Cooperstown Room

Learn about the Museum's origins, the history of the National Baseball Hall of Fame and Museum, and Cooperstown's formative role in the national pastime.

# Grandstand Theater

Prepare for an emotional journey through baseball history with *The Baseball Experience*, an entertaining thirteen-minute all-digital multimedia presentation in the Museum's main theater.

# Taking the Field
## *The 19th Century*

*Taking the Field: The 19th Century* offers a comprehensive examination of baseball's origins and early clubs, featuring more than 150 artifacts and graphics.

The exhibit spotlights several hands-on activities. Visitors can leaf through a scrapbook of a century of worldwide baseball tours. A stereoscope depicts authentic baseball scenes from the nineteenth century. Visitors can also use a telegraph key to tap out baseball plays in Morse code, just as newspaper reporters did in the second half of the century.

Ambient nineteenth-century baseball music complements the exhibit, while a video presentation of baseball plays, re-created by period performers, illustrates nineteenth-century baseball rules. Custom-made Victorian wallpaper, produced by the American Paper-Staining Manufactory at the Farmers' Museum in Cooperstown, adorns the exhibit walls.

ABOVE: The entrance to Taking the Field: The 19th Century greets visitors with the Eckford Ball Case (FAR LEFT), featuring baseballs from the Eckford club of the mid-1800s.

Partially legible exhibit text:

ter Joe McCarthy, the New
n a dominant run in 1936
en pennants and six world
eight years.

NEW YORK

**Yanks Return**

New York Yankees resumed their mastery
American League throughout the late 1930s
arly 1940s. The Yankees were the first team
n four consecutive World Series, winning
year from 1936 to 1939. This era of Yankees
ory is marked by the dominance and then
den decline of Lou Gehrig and the emergence
uperstar Joe DiMaggio.

*"He was a symbol of indestructibility—
a Gibraltar in cleats."*
—Sports columnist Jim Murray

45
CRACKS
RECORD

# The Game: Baseball's Time Line

Learn about the game's greatest teams, players, moments, and stories through original
artifacts, compelling photographs, and classic ephemera, with a chronological presentation
of baseball history.

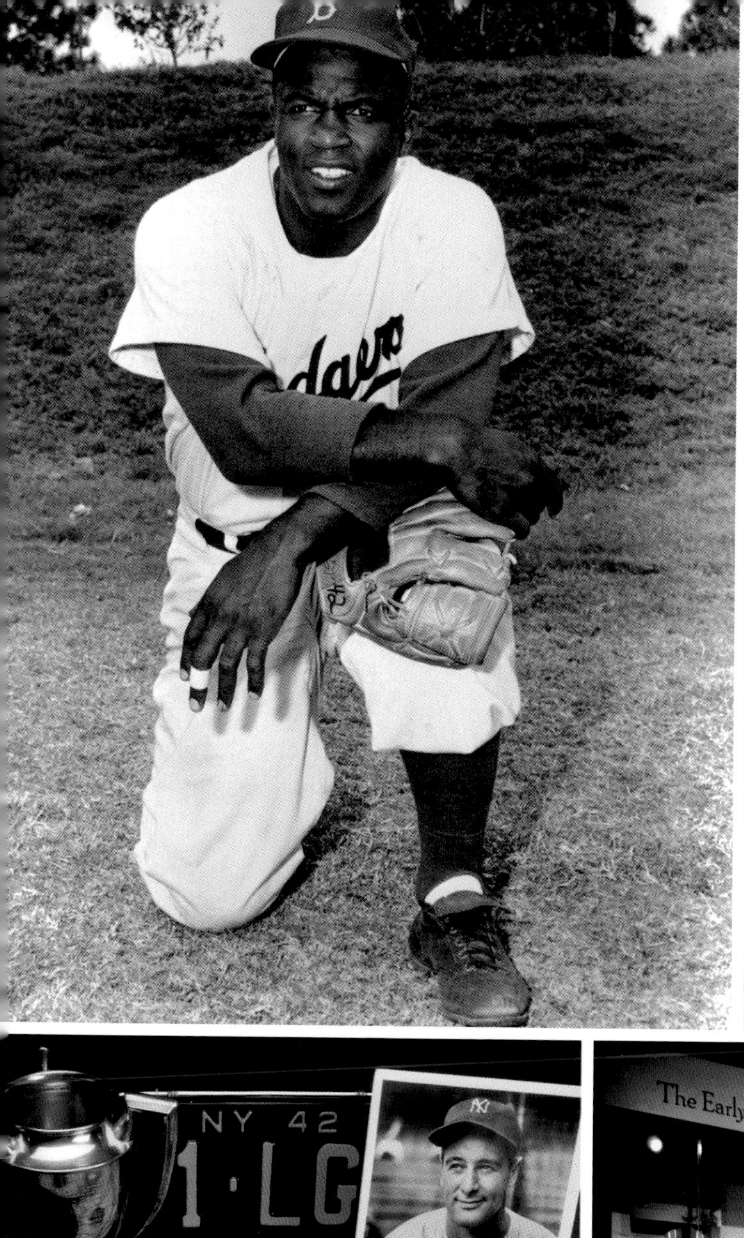

NY 42
1·LG
GENUINE
Lou Gehrig
LOUISVILLE SLUGGER
LOU GEHRIG

The Early Glory Days
NATIONAL LEAGUE

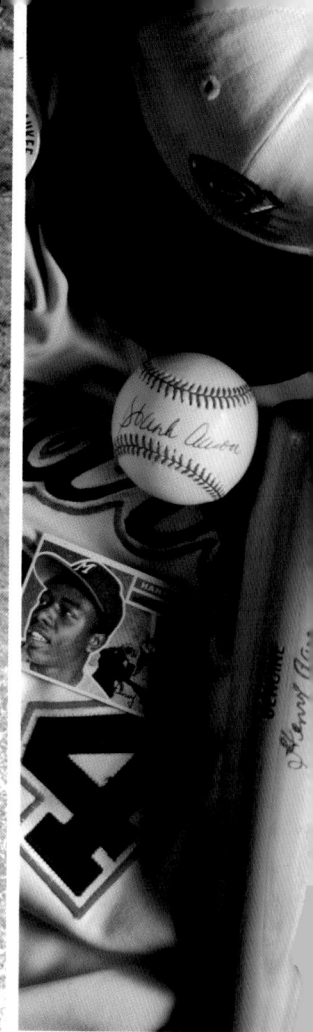

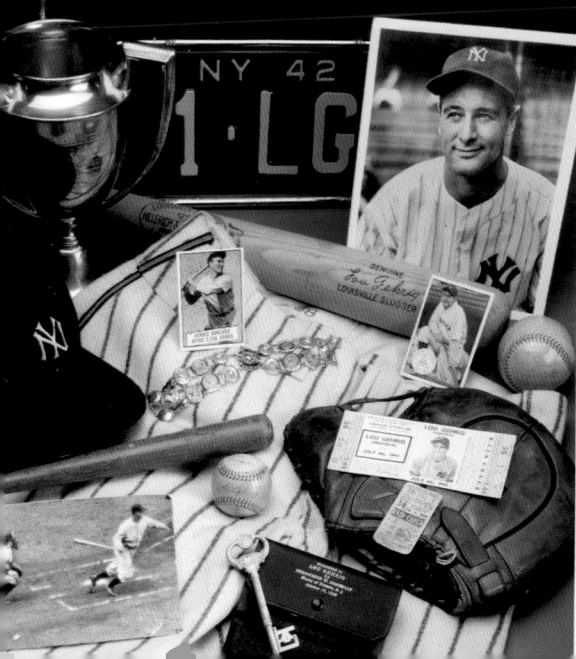

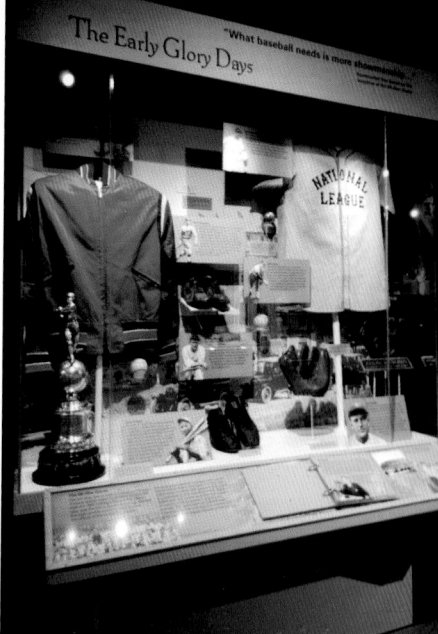

# Babe Ruth Gallery

Baseball's first superstar, Babe Ruth, revolutionized the sport with his monster swing and larger-than-life personality. In this gallery, learn about George Herman "Babe" Ruth, the player and the man.

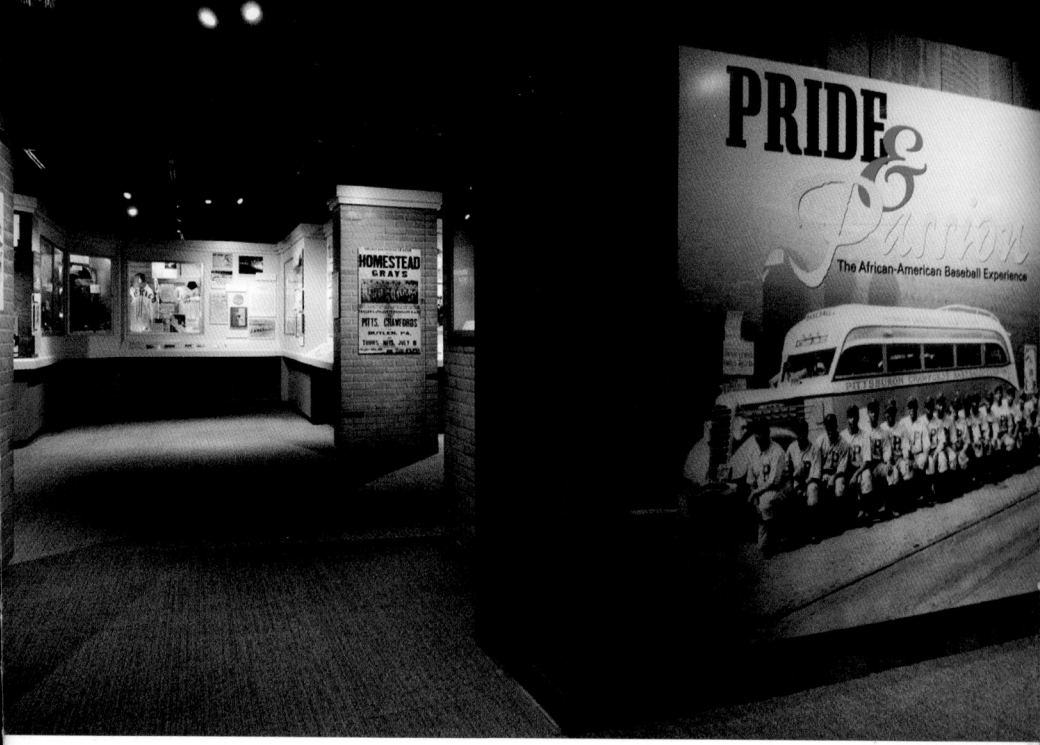

# Pride and Passion
## *The African American Baseball Experience*

Dedicated to the men and women whose passion for our national game helped them triumph over obstacles brought about by prejudice and intolerance in our nation, this exhibit recognizes the contributions of African Americans in baseball.

The exhibit pays tribute to 100 years of African-American involvement in baseball, from Civil War days through integration, with special recognition of the legacy of Hall of Famer Jackie Robinson, whose actions on and off the field served as a catalyst for progress.

The exhibit features lessons on creating opportunity, barnstorming teams and players, separate leagues, the evolution of the famed Negro Leagues, challenges for the Negro Leagues when African Americans joined the major league ranks, and the post-integration era of African Americans in executive and managerial roles in the game.

Artifacts include awards, documents, uniforms, and equipment from stars such as Jackie Robinson, Satchel Paige, Buck Leonard, and Frank Robinson.

OPPOSITE: Kansas City Monarchs star pitcher Satchel Paige, a member of the Baseball Hall of Fame. ABOVE: The *Pride and Passion* exhibit honoring African-American contributions to baseball.

# Diamond Dreams
*Women in Baseball*

The contributions of women pioneers to the game are celebrated and revered in one of the Museum's most popular exhibits. Featuring the memories and stars of the All-American Girls Professional Baseball League (AAGPBL) and high-lighted by the feats of other women on and off the field, the Museum's *Diamond Dreams* exhibit details the significant impact women have had on the game.

The original exhibit helped establish the story line for the 1992 theatrical re-lease *A League of Their Own*, and many of the stories from the real-life league, as well as the movie, are on display. Learn about pioneers such as Alta Weiss, Ila Borders, and other women who have left their mark on our national pastime.

OPPOSITE: Artifacts from the All-American Girls Professional Baseball League. ABOVE: *The Diamond Dreams: Women in Baseball* exhibit.

# Viva Baseball

*¡Viva Baseball!* celebrates the Latin American impact on
baseball through an interactive presentation and documen-
tation of Caribbean Basin countries and players.

The exhibit features nearly 150 artifacts and a state-
of-the-art multi-media presentation celebrating the Latin
love affair with baseball, spanning nearly 150 years of
history. The exhibit focuses on the rich baseball traditions
of the Caribbean, and how the joy, flair and passion for the
game has enriched the sport in the United States.

# Today's Game

*Today's Game* combines the Museum's most recent artifact acquisitions with video highlights to re-create the look and feel of a major league clubhouse.

*Today's Game* features more than 250 artifacts from the last ten baseball seasons, with a locker dedicated to each of the 30 major league teams. Artifacts from historical achievements of each current major league season fill the center cases of the exhibit.

Each major league team is represented with artifacts from the last ten seasons in the *Today's Game* exhibit.

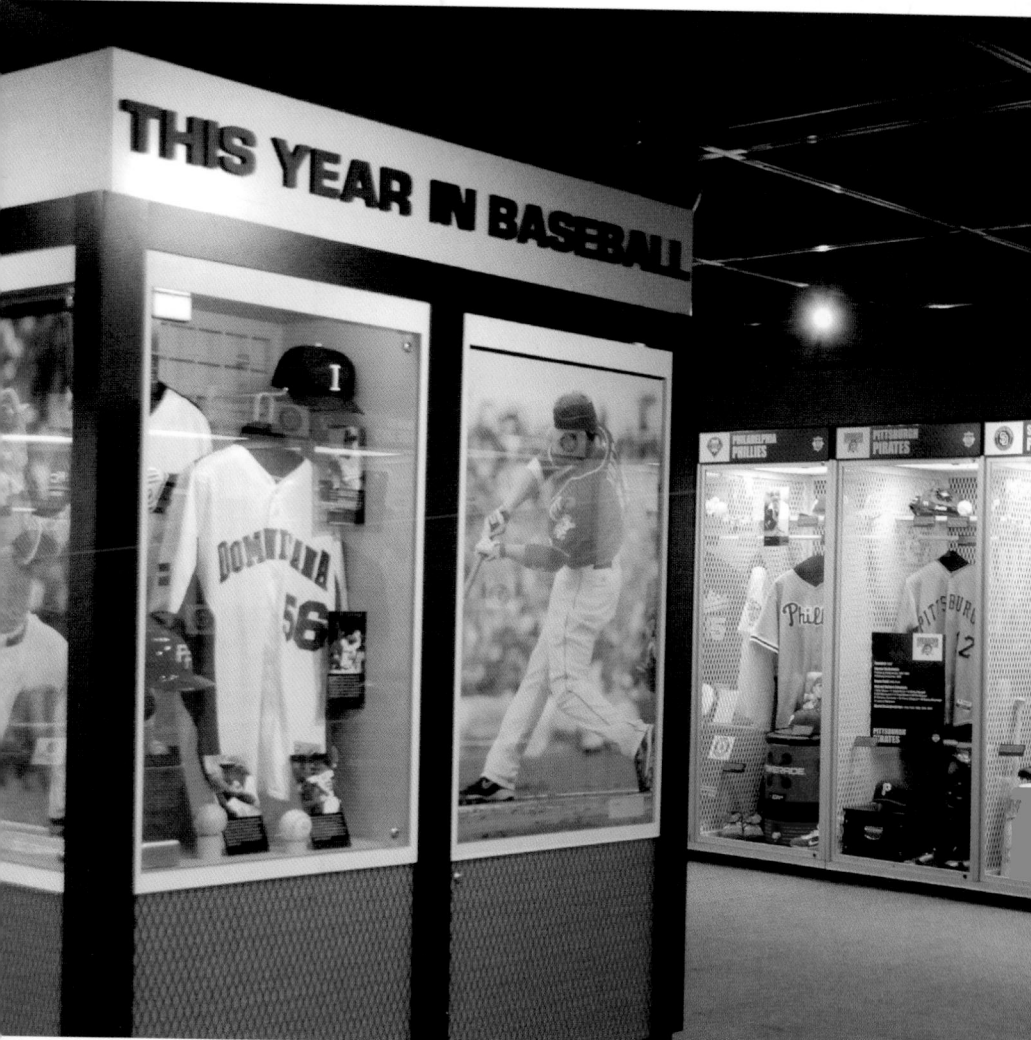

Fabric mâché statues of favorite fans at ballparks across the country greet visitors at the third-floor entrance to *Sacred Ground*, the Museum's exhibit dedicated to ballparks and the fan experience.

# Third Floor

# Sacred Ground

*Sacred Ground* explores the ballparks of our great game's past and present, with more than 200 artifacts documenting the fan experience at baseball's hallowed fields of green.

Among the most notable artifacts in the exhibit are a scoreboard pinwheel from Comiskey Park, a ticket booth from Yankee Stadium, a turnstile from the Polo Grounds, the cornerstone from Ebbets Field, Walter Johnson's locker from Griffith Stadium, and the Pittsburgh Pirates on-deck circle from Forbes Field.

The exhibit also includes a special interactive section dedicated to music at the ballpark. Visitors can hear the distinctive sounds from various ballparks and learn the history of the classic baseball song "Take Me Out to the Ball Game."

Ballparks of the past come to life in *Sacred Ground* with the sights and sounds of the National Pastime preserved in this popular exhibit, which takes visitors to scene of some of baseball's most memorable moments.

ABOVE: The cornerstone from Ebbets Field, in Brooklyn, N.Y. OPPOSITE TOP: A famed scoreboard pinwheel from Chicago's Comiskey Park. OPPOSITE BOTTOM: *Sacred Ground* celebrates the fan experience.

# Chasing the Dream

*Hank Aaron: Chasing the Dream* chronicles Hank Aaron's life, from childhood through the big leagues and his post-baseball career, including his vast philanthropic efforts.

Aaron played 23 seasons for the Milwaukee and Atlanta Braves and the Milwaukee Brewers. He fought racism to become the all-time home run champion, a record that stood for more than 30 years, and was one of the most consistent offensive powers in the game. He totaled 3,771 hits, 755 home runs, holds major league records for extra-base hits and RBI and was selected to 25 All-Star Games. Aaron won the 1957 National League Most Valuable Player Award and won three Gold Glove Awards for his play in right field. He was inducted into the National Baseball Hall of Fame in 1982.

# One for the Books

The players set the standards. The numbers became iconic. The stories are now legend.

But it's the records that enthrall baseball fans the world over—from Cy Young's victories to Joe DiMaggio's 56-game hitting streak to Cal Ripken's consistent appearance in the box score. Those records remain forever a part of the National Pastime.

The records—and the stories forever connected to them—are celebrated in this exhibit.

*One for the Books: Baseball Records and the Stories Behind Them* represents a landmark permanent exhibit. *One for the Books* tell the story baseball's most cherished records through more than 200 artifacts in the most technologically advanced presentation in the Museum's history.

Chicago
23
PIRATES

2013
WORLD SERIES
FP
5
UNDER ARMOUR
marucci
David Ortiz

# Autumn Glory
## *A Postseason Celebration*

*Autumn Glory* commemorates more than 100 years of postseason play and World Series memories. Featuring artifacts, documents, photographs and interactive displays, the 2,400-square foot exhibit highlights numerous classic postseason moments and baseball's October heroes. From the last-out ball of the first modern World Series in 1903 to artifacts from the most recent Fall Classic, every October is represented through iconic pieces and interactive stories.

The exhibit contains hundreds of postseason game-related items, including World Championship trophies; the bat used by Joe Carter to hit is walk-off home run in the 1993 World Series; World Series jewelry such as championship rings, charms, pendants and press pins; and an exhibit dedicated to the most recent World Series champion.

The exhibit also features the video story of past World Series winners, and interactive displays that allow visitors to access World Series statistics, records and recaps. A tribute case to the current World Champions is updated annually.

OPPOSITE: *Autumn Glory* features artifacts from the first modern World Series in 1903 through the most recent Fall Classic. ABOVE: World Series ring and press pin presented to the Cincinnati Reds after winning the 1975 World Series.

# Who's On First?

One of the Museum's most popular inclusions, the classic Bud Abbott and Lou Costello comedy routine of "Who's On First?" has mesmerized generations of visitors to the Hall of Fame. Located on the Museum's third floor, the video routine remains indelibly marked into the American psyche.

Artwork ranging from paintings to sculptures can be found in the Museum's *Art of Baseball* exhibit.

# First Floor

# Inductee Row

See artifacts from the current class of Hall of Fame inductees and relive their historic careers. BELOW TOP: Cal Ripken Jr. and Tony Gwynn share their Hall of Fame induction moment during Hall of Fame Weekend 2007. BELOW BOTTOM: The 2013 class of inductees are celebrated through artifacts and images.

# The Frank and Peggy Steele Art Gallery

Original works of art—paintings, sculptures, and prints—underline America's love affair with baseball.

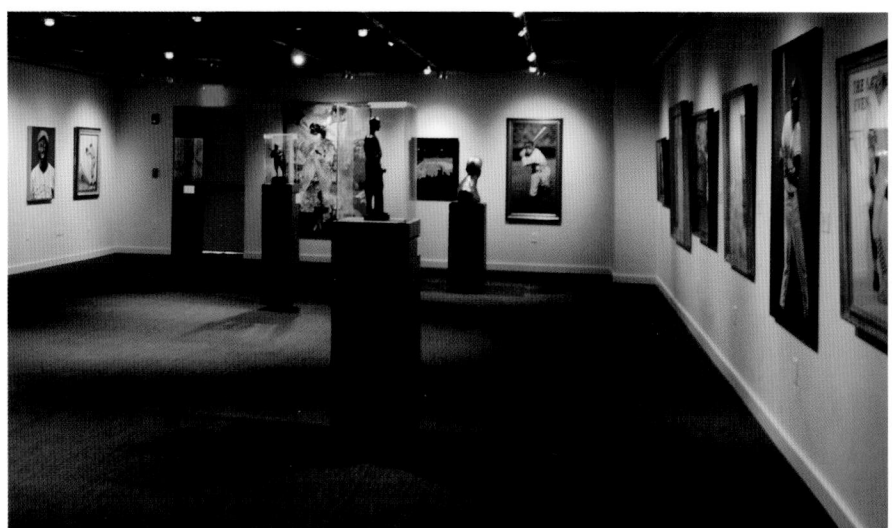

# Scribes and Mikemen

Hear famed audio recordings of baseball's memorable moments while learning about the winners of the prestigious Ford C. Frick and J. G. Taylor Spink awards, presented annually to a baseball broadcaster and writer, respectively.

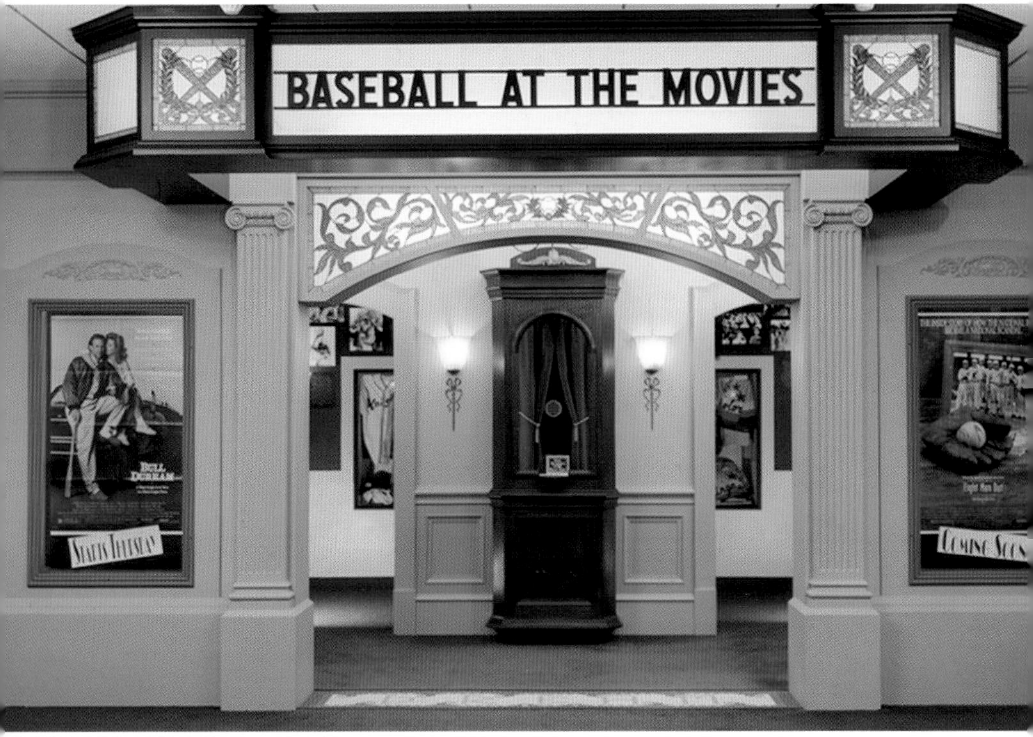

# Baseball at the Movies

Explore the intimate relationship that baseball and Hollywood have shared through the years with artifacts from cinema blockbusters and pop culture favorites, including the jacket and cap worn by Robert Redford in *The Natural* (BOTTOM, LEFT) and costume tunics worn during the filming of *A League of Their Own* (BOTTOM, RIGHT).

# Reaching BASE

**'Be A Superior Example'**
**Program Encourages All**
**to Live Free of Performance-**
**Enhancing Substances**

The National Baseball Hall of Fame and Museum's connection to education—and the ability to inspire young minds with important lessons of American culture through the lens of baseball—has been a defining hallmark of the spiritual home for the game for a generation of learners.

In 2012, a new era in the Museum's education realm arrived, with the introduction of a national initiative designed to promote healthy habits for individuals of all ages.

The "Be A Superior Example" program, known by its acronym "BASE," draws from health sciences curriculum, while promoting the benefit of four foundations—fitness, nutrition, character and fair play—to represent each of the four bases on the diamond.

The comprehensive trip around the bases makes the content unique, and it is in crossing home plate—where all participants are then provided an opportunity to pledge to live and play free of performance-enhancing substances—that signifies an historic first for Cooperstown, a social program designed to provide a roadmap for individuals of all ages in understanding the harmful impact of

steroids, in our game and in communities across the country.

"The BASE program promotes healthy choices, while educating students and adults about the dangers of performance-enhancing substances," said Hall of Fame President Jeff Idelson. "The introduction of this content to the Museum's award-winning educational curriculum is a natural integration into how we educate youth everyday about American culture, with topics ranging from history and character education to math and science. BASE provides a powerful refrain and common foundation for students of all ages that performance-enhancing substances are dangerous, and the only way to live a healthy life is to do so free of these harmful substances. It can be accessed online at baseballhall.org/BASE and through interactive kiosks located in the Museum's Library Atrium."

# The National Baseball Hall of Fame Library

The National Baseball Hall of Fame Library was founded in 1939 as part of the National Baseball Hall of Fame and Museum. Its mission is to collect, organize, and preserve the complete history of our national pastime as recorded in all media formats for the use of baseball fans and researchers.

The collection at the Library has been acquired through the generosity of baseball fans, researchers, teams, and players. Donors are accorded special recognition and privileges. If you would like to help us document our national pastime and preserve its heritage for future generations, please consider becoming a donor.

## The A. Bartlett Giamatti Research Center

The A. Bartlett Giamatti Research Center, rededicated in memory of the former commissioner of baseball on July 26, 1998, can help you find answers to your baseball questions, large or small. Our vast collection of baseball books, magazines, newspaper clippings, and archival material is a rich source of information on baseball and related topics.

Today, the Library contains the world's most extensive collec-

tion of archival material devoted exclusively to baseball. This is a public facility, and thousands of researchers, Museum visitors, callers, and correspondents are served annually.

The Library is open from 9 A.M. until 5 P.M. weekdays from March through October. From November through February, the Library is open Wednesdays, Thursdays, and Fridays from 9 A.M. to 5 P.M. On-site appointments and off-site research assistance can be arranged by calling (607) 547-0330.

## Recorded Media Department

The Library contains more than 14,000 hours of moving image and sound recordings. The collection includes interviews, game highlights, television and radio broadcasts,

animation, and music. Selections from the collection are featured daily in the Museum's Bullpen Theater.

Many of the selections within the Library's Recorded Media Department are available for purchase from the Hall of Fame.

For more information, please call (607) 547-0330.

## Photo Archive

More than 250,000 original images of players, teams, stadiums, events and other subjects are housed in the Library.

The collection includes black-and-white prints, color prints, slides, transparencies and negatives.

Many of the photographs in the collection are available for reproduction. We will gladly send a limited selection of photocopies for review. Please note that a research fee may be charged for extensive requests. All photograph reproduction rates are per image and are subject to change. Orders may be paid by check, money order or credit card.

To contact the Photo Archive, please call (607) 547-0375.

The Hall of Fame Library features more than three million documents, including more than 14,000 hours of recorded audio and video.

# The Earliest Artifacts

**Alexander Cleland, with the help
of Hall of Famers like Cy Young, laid
the groundwork for the Museum's
incomparable collection of artifacts.**

A few years prior to the official
dedication of the National Baseball Hall
of Fame and Museum in 1939, the individual charged with the task of acquiring
artifacts for the new institution found
himself in a bit of a quandary.

"I hate to offer alibis for the slow
progress we are making, but it seems as
if something always happens to upset the
plans I make," wrote Alexander Cleland,
the executive secretary of the recently
established National Baseball Museum,
to Walter Littell, the editor of *The Otsego
Farmer*, a Cooperstown newspaper, in
a letter dated June 13, 1935. "Mr. Ford
Frick, the President of the National
League, agreed to approach Judge Fuchs
[owner of the Boston Braves] to try to
secure a baseball suit and other material
belonging to Babe Ruth. The quarrel
between Judge Fuchs and Babe Ruth
spoiled that plan and I will have to try
something else.

"It may be a little difficult to make
the average person understand how slow
it is to get a Museum like this started.

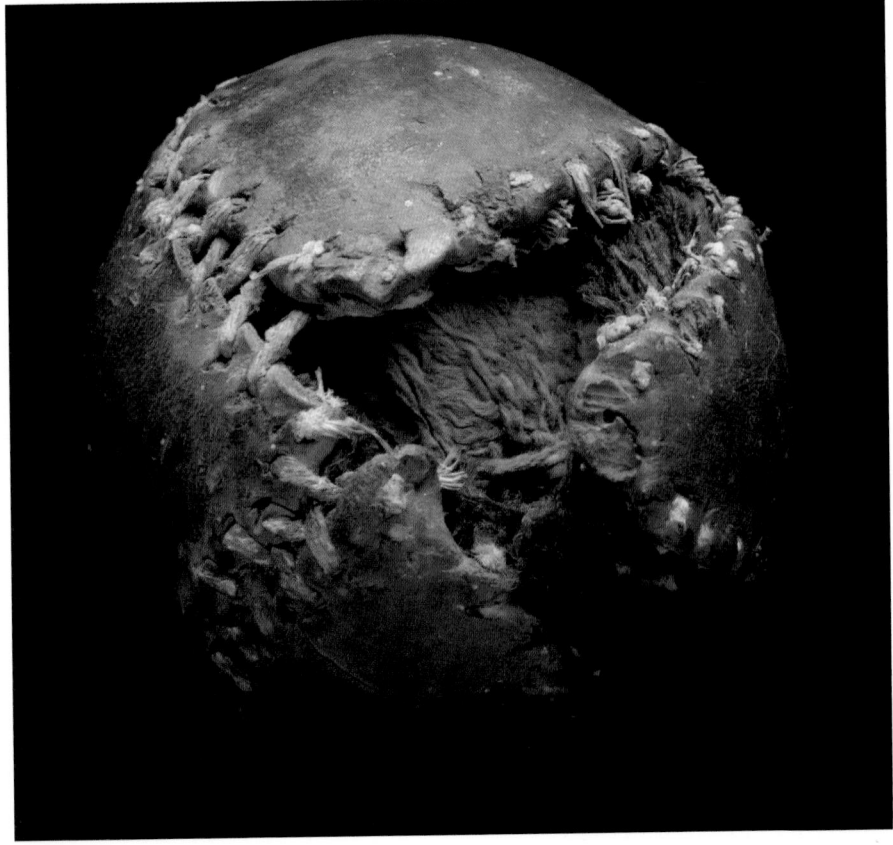

Unique artifacts in the Museum's collections include (OPPOSITE LEFT) the Doubleday Baseball, a homemade ball found in a home a few miles up the road from Cooperstown in the village of Fly Creek, N.Y.; (ABOVE) and treasures from Cy Young, whose donations in the Museum's earliest days help establish the Cooperstown shrine as the home for the National Pastime's artifacts.

One of the difficulties is that many of them take the attitude that the Centennial is not until 1939 and therefore there is no great hurry in the matter. However, I am quite sure that if we keep plugging away we will ultimately have a worthwhile collection."

"Plugging away" is exactly what Cleland kept doing. Seventy-five years later, the seeds sown by Cleland have blossomed into a Museum known throughout the world and the cornerstone of the home of baseball.

A native of Glasgow, Scotland, Cleland was hired by Stephen C. Clark, a Cooperstown resident and philanthropist, in 1931 to be the director of Clark House, established in New York City to provide services for immigrants.

Soon after a 1934 meeting with Clark in Cooperstown on matters concerning Clark House, Cleland wrote to his boss of an encounter with a Doubleday Field worker.

"A young man very enthusiastically asked me what I thought of the field and told me Cooperstown was looking forward with great interest to 1939 because they were planning a celebration of the 100th anniversary of Baseball.

"Thinking the matter over coming down on the train I wondered if it would not be possible to bring many visitors to Cooperstown before that time and get a large amount of publicity thru the following plan:

"Interest the Baseball Writers Association in promoting a building on

ABOVE: Ty Cobb, one of the first five electees to the Hall of Fame, donated several artifacts to the Museum representing his legendary exploits on the diamond. OPPOSITE: The Museum's collection spans the decades of artifacts, and includes items like this panel used to control the scoreboard at Houston's Astrodome.

Doubleday Field where a collection of all past, present and future historical data of the game could be shown. There must be in the country a great many valuable pictures and material that would make an interesting museum. Besides pictures, funny old uniforms, the baseballs thrown out and autographed by the various Presidents and the famous bats of players like Ruth, Cobb, Hornsby, etc. I will not elaborate further, but I could suggest scores of interesting things for the lovers of baseball."

Cleland's idea began to take hold in April 1935, when a farmer living in Fly Creek, a crossroads village three miles from Cooperstown, came across an ancient trunk in his attic where it had gone untouched for generations. In it were the belongings of Abner Graves, the one who testified in later life that the game of baseball was invented in Cooperstown by Abner Doubleday.

The trunk included an antique baseball, undersized, misshapen and obviously homemade. Its interior exposed, it had cloth stuffing rather than the tightly wound twine of the modern ball. Clark purchased the "Doubleday Baseball" for $5 and placed it, along with other artifacts, on exhibit in the Village Club, a building that sits on the corner of Main and Fair streets today. He hoped the exhibit would draw visitors to Cooperstown.

Cooperstown village leaders eventually assembled in 1935 and organized the National Baseball Museum "for the purpose of collecting and preserving pictures and relics reflecting the development of the National Game from the time of its inception, through the ingenuity of Major General Abner Doubleday, in 1839 to the present."

Cleland, possessing great imagination and unbounded energy, was elected official secretary to proceed with full authority in acquiring baseball artifacts. Important early acquisitions came from Ford Frick, Washington Senators owner Clark Griffith, the widows of Christy Mathewson and John McGraw and the families of sporting good magnates Benjamin Shibe and Al Reach.

But Cleland's enthusiasm and tenacity was on full display when he sent identical letters, dated Feb. 18, 1937, to such recent Hall of Fame electees as Honus Wagner, Cy Young, Tris Speaker, Napoleon Lajoie, Ty Cobb and Babe Ruth, stating, in part, "we wish to secure some mementoes for the museum from those who are in the Hall of Fame. I am, therefore, writing to inquire if you will be good enough to donate to the Museum any reminders of your baseball days, such as baseballs, bats, suit, or any other souvenirs that might be of interest to the baseball fan when he visits the museum.

"I trust you will cooperate with us to the end, that the Hall of Fame will not only show the busts and plaques of great players, but also that the museum will contain personal affects of the players in connection with their own association with the game."

Among the first to respond to Cleland's plea was Young, who, on Feb. 28, 1937, wrote, "Sure I will donate. I have quite a lot of pictures I could send you. I have a baseball that I used in Washington, D.C. 1908 when I won my 500th game. I have some very valuable cups, also my last uniform while with the Boston Braves in 1911. I feel sure I can make you a fine collection. My cups I received while with the Boston Red Sox."

Today, thanks in part to the early efforts of Cleland, there are more than 40,000 artifacts in the Museum's collection, including 7,000 baseballs, 2,000 bats, 1,000 uniforms, 750 caps, 500 gloves and 300 pair of shoes/spikes.

Together, they tell the story of the National Pastime—a story preserved for all time in Cooperstown.

# Higher Learning

**Education Programs Evolve Into Institutional Calling Card as Lens for American Culture**

The starting lineup for the National Baseball Hall of Fame and Museum features the biggest names in the history of the game. Individually, each has the ability to generate wins. But together, they have limitless potential to bring victory to individuals of all ages, through a variety of skill sets that make them among the best.

*Inspire. Explore. Enrich. Engage. Encourage. Lead. Captivate. Share. Connect.*

These words reflect the Hall of Fame spirit seen everyday in education programs delivered on-site in Cooperstown or through distance-learning initiatives to audiences throughout the Americas. Since 1991, education has been a central focus for the Museum in sharing the valuable lessons which baseball offers beyond the diamond in its role in reflecting and shaping American culture and history.

The Museum's impact on reaching school children with thematic explora-tions of baseball has never been more important.

With the introduction of the "Be A Superior Example" (BASE) program in 2012, the Museum now features 17 areas of emphasis for examining the role baseball plays in our society. These lessons, designed for educator-led K-12 audiences, and adapted for in-Museum public programs throughout the calendar year, provide foundational and social messages and learning modules.

More than two decades since the Hall of Fame first launched an educational program, the institutional goals for the future are focused on building outreach, awareness and visibility—using technology, original collection assets, and an award-winning curriculum deliver a more dynamic learning experience.

In the first years of the new century, videoconferencing technology provided a game-changing opportunity for the Hall of Fame, through federal government appropriation funding in 2004. Through

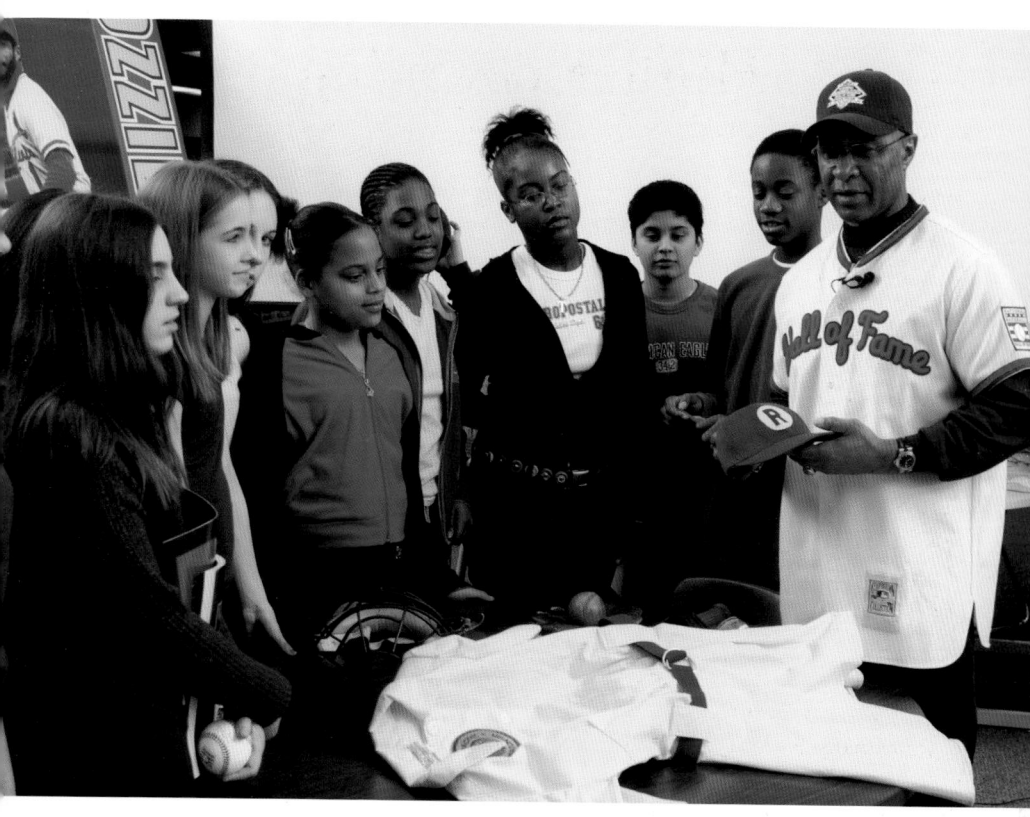

Hall of Fame Education Ambassador Ozzie Smith teaches a group of St. Louis area students about the history of uniforms and the role of women in baseball.

this initiative, more than 75,000 students have connected virtually through standard classroom settings, providing an intimate educational experience with communities all across the country.

School kids from coast-to-coast have had the opportunity to visit Cooperstown without even leaving their desks or their classrooms.

Over the last three years, the Museum's education modules have been adapted for audiences for all grades, K-12. With 17 modules in areas of math, science, social studies, arts, character education, and health science, the Museum provides engaging and entertaining educational opportunities, both in Cooperstown and around the globe, with

four full-time education staff members and nearly 20 part-time educators.

Curriculum for all of the Museum's programs now offers lesson plans for audiences from K-12 and beyond. As schools adapt to Core Curriculum standards nationally, the Hall of Fame is positioned to be a leader in interactive and immersive education.

The Museum's videoconferencing program has captured national recognition for high praise received from teachers for the institution's educational value and interactivity. On-site audiences are the beneficiaries of innovative programming and exposures to enlighten audiences from across New York State and from around the Northeast.

# Sandlot Kids' Clubhouse

The Sandlot Kids' Clubhouse features more than fifteen youth-friendly experiences. The exhibit contains many interactive components such as a magnetic game called Batter Up! that teaches baseball fielding positions and mathematical concepts. A vertical measurement chart represents the heights of several famous players from the major leagues, Negro leagues, and the All-American Girls Professional Baseball League (AAGPBL).

In the discovery area, visitors can rummage through discovery drawers filled with Museum artifacts. A signature feature of the discovery area is an interactive literacy corner called What's On Next. There, a 37-inch flat-panel LCD screen features several programs, including a message from Hall of Famer and Museum Educational Ambassador Ozzie Smith; *Curious George Plays Baseball*, narrated by Hall of Fame member Brooks Robinson; and *Players in Pigtails*, narrated by AAGPBL veteran Terry Donahue. Additionally, *Garfield* creator Jim Davis has contributed a rendering of the cartoon cat dressed as a ballpark vendor.

The Sandlot Kids Clubhouse is located on the Museum's first floor adjacent to the Library Atrium.

The Sandlot Kids' Clubhouse provides an educational experience for visitors ages 4–10.

# Baseball History on the Web

## *Stay Connected to Cooperstown Year-Round*

The National Baseball Hall of Fame and Museum comes to life online with baseball history. Baseballhall.org is the official home of the Hall of Fame online, with everything you've ever wanted to know about our national pastime centrally located for fans of the game.

The website features online exhibits, bios, and compelling content on every Hall of Fame member, in addition to news from Cooperstown, tips for planning your visit, and so much more. The Museum's website also features original video productions, stories and features in-depth looks at the history of our National Pastime.

Hall of Fame plaques are available for viewing, along with research lists for baseball fans of every era to enjoy.

Stay connected to Cooperstown through the Museum's social media outlets on Facebook (www.facebook.com/baseballhall); Twitter (www.twitter.com/baseballhall); YouTube (www.youtube.com/thebaseballhall); and Instagram (www.instagram.com/baseballhall).Visit baseballhall.org to sign up for the best lineup of baseball history, delivered right to your computer or mobile device.

# Around Cooperstown

Cooperstown is more than just baseball. Its Main Street way of life is supported by two additional world-class museums, a nationally renowned summer opera, a beautiful 9-mile-long lake, and deep historical roots that served as the basis for the novels of James Fenimore Cooper and his Leatherstocking Tales.

With a year-round population of just over 2,000 residents, the village of Cooperstown offers the simplicities of an earlier era. No large shopping malls can be found in the area, and the warm sense of community, bordered by the wooded hills and Otsego Lake, keep the region one of America's most treasured jewels.

Other attractions dot the landscape, providing the ultimate vacation destination for a wide range of travelers. Whether you are looking for a weekend getaway or a summer in paradise, be sure you visit these other village attractions.

**The Otesaga Resort Hotel** One of New York State's most distinctive resorts, The Otesaga has operated since 1909 and is a member of the prestigious Historic Hotels of America. It is noted for its distinguished service, fine dining, championship Leatherstocking Golf Course, and beautiful views. Visit otesaga.com.

**Fenimore Art Museum** This elegant 1930s neo-Georgian mansion features a showcase of premier collections of American art, including the acclaimed Eugene and Clare Thaw Collection of North American Indian Art. Visit fenimoreartmuseum.org.

**The Farmers' Museum** Step back in time and experience New York State history, where skilled artisans practice the trades and crafts of the nineteenth century. See authentically restored historic buildings and period furnishings, heritage gardens, rare breeds of farm animals, and more. Visit farmersmuseum.org.

**Doubleday Field** Operated by the village of Cooperstown, Doubleday Field hosts more than 300 baseball games annually at every level of competition.

For more information on the village of Cooperstown and the year-round schedule of events and activities, please contact the Cooperstown Chamber of Commerce by phone at (607) 547-9931 or via the Web at cooperstownchamber.org.

# How to Support
# the Hall of Fame

**Preserving History. Honoring Excellence.
Connecting Generations.**

*The Mission of the National Baseball
Hall of Fame and Museum*

The National Baseball Hall of Fame and
Museum is an educational institution
dedicated to fostering an appreciation
of the historical development of baseball
and its impact on our culture, through
collecting, preserving, exhibiting, and
interpreting its collections for a global
audience, as well as honoring those who
have made outstanding contributions to
the sport.

## Supporting the Hall of Fame

As a nonprofit organization, independent
of Major League Baseball, the Hall of
Fame depends on support from a variety
of sources and at many different levels to
maintain its operations. Since its official
opening in 1939, it has been the Museum's practice to accept only donated
artifacts.

The Hall of Fame welcomes mone-
tary gifts ranging from annual fund gifts,
matching funds, endowment giving,
bequests, and more. For information on
how you can support the Hall of Fame,
please contact the development office at
(607) 547-0333.

## Membership Program

The most convenient way to support the
National Baseball Hall of Fame and Museum is to become a member. Members
receive benefits at a variety of levels, while
helping to support the Hall of Fame's mission and educational programs. Individual
memberships start at $50.

Benefits of becoming a member
include a subscription to *Memories and
Dreams* magazine, the official publication
of the National Baseball Hall of Fame
and Museum, published six times per
year; the annual Hall of Fame Yearbook,
featuring bios of Hall of Fame members;
free shipping and 10 percent off retail
purchases made on-site and online;
and free admission to the Museum
throughout the year.

For higher levels of membership,
opportunities are available, including
reserved Induction Ceremony seating;
special event access with Hall of Fame
members; and limited edition gifts, such
as lithographs and paintings.

You can learn more today by visiting
the Membership Desk in the Museum
lobby, enrolling online at baseballhall.org,
or calling (607) 547-0397.

OPPOSITE: The Otesaga Resort Hotel in Cooperstown.

# Hall of Fame Events

**Baseball's Legends Return Each July**

The signature special event of the National Baseball Hall of Fame and Museum, Hall of Fame Weekend offers visitors to Cooperstown an opportunity to see the largest congregation of living legends, while honoring the newest electees to the sport's greatest shrine. Held the final weekend in July every year, Hall of Fame Weekend provides entertainment for fans of all ages, highlighted by the Induction Ceremony on Sunday, in which fifty to sixty Hall of Famers return to welcome the newest inductees. The Saturday Awards Presentation features the honoring of the J.G. Taylor Spink Award winner (for writers) and the Ford C. Frick Award winner (for broadcasters).

Activities abound for fans of all ages, ranging from a Youth Skills Clinic at Doubleday Field to the Main Street Game Day Parade.

**Hall of Fame Classic**

The Museum hosts "Hall of Fame Classic," a Legends game, on Memorial Day Weekend. The Classic features Hall of Famers as well as nearly 30 other former major league players at historic Doubleday Field. A parade, interactive programs, "Night at the Museum" experience and fundraising golf tournament supports the game, which features a salute to the long-standing relationship between baseball history and the Armed Services.

The Major League Baseball Players Alumni Association serves as an additional participant in the Classic game by identifying players and hosting a Skills Clinic.

Ford Motor Company is the presenting sponsor for the Hall of Fame Classic and Classic Weekend.

**Programming Activities and Special Events**

The Museum offers more than 1,000 programming events over the course of the year, ranging from the All-Star Game and World Series galas to rookie workshops designed for the young visitor. Daily programming runs throughout the summer months, with special events, anniversary celebrations, and activities for visitors of all ages scheduled year-round.

Hall of Famers Ozzie Smith and Phil Niekro ride down Main Street in Cooperstown in the Hall of Fame Classic Game Day Parade.

# Take Cooperstown
# Home with You

## Museum Store

The Museum Store is located on the first floor and provides a fitting ending to your Hall of Fame journey. Visit the Store for unique gifts, keepsakes, and apparel for yourself and the baseball fans in your life. Your purchases help support the Hall of Fame and its not-for-profit educational mission.

While visiting the Museum Store, sign up to receive a merchandise catalog; *Inside Pitch*, the Hall of Fame's free weekly e-mail newsletter; and a trial copy of *Memories and Dreams*, the Hall of Fame's official magazine.

## Museum Bookstore

Also be sure to visit the Museum Bookstore, located in the Library Atrium, which carries a wide variety of books and videos on many baseball subjects. Popular book signings take place in the adjacent Library Atrium year-round, and signed books and many others can be purchased from the Bookstore.

## Photo Collection

The National Baseball Hall of Fame Library contains nearly 250,000 original photographs detailing the game's illustrious history, from the 1840s to today.

Featuring Hall of Famers, teams, stadiums, historic events, players, Negro league stars, the AAGPBL, and others, the collection's rich selection of photos appeals to fans of all eras of our national game. Each photo offered is a reprint of the original image in the permanent collection of the Hall of Fame Library.

Order images in the Museum Store, online at baseballhall.org, or by calling (607) 547-0375.

## Discovery Tour

A motivating Discovery Tour leads young baseball fans and their families through the Museum together in search of answers to enlightening trivia questions. A rich combination of education and timeless artifacts provides for great fun and reminiscing.

ABOVE: Photographs from the Hall of Fame's collection are available at the Museum Store.

# Photo Credits

Plaque commemorating the first induction in 1939.